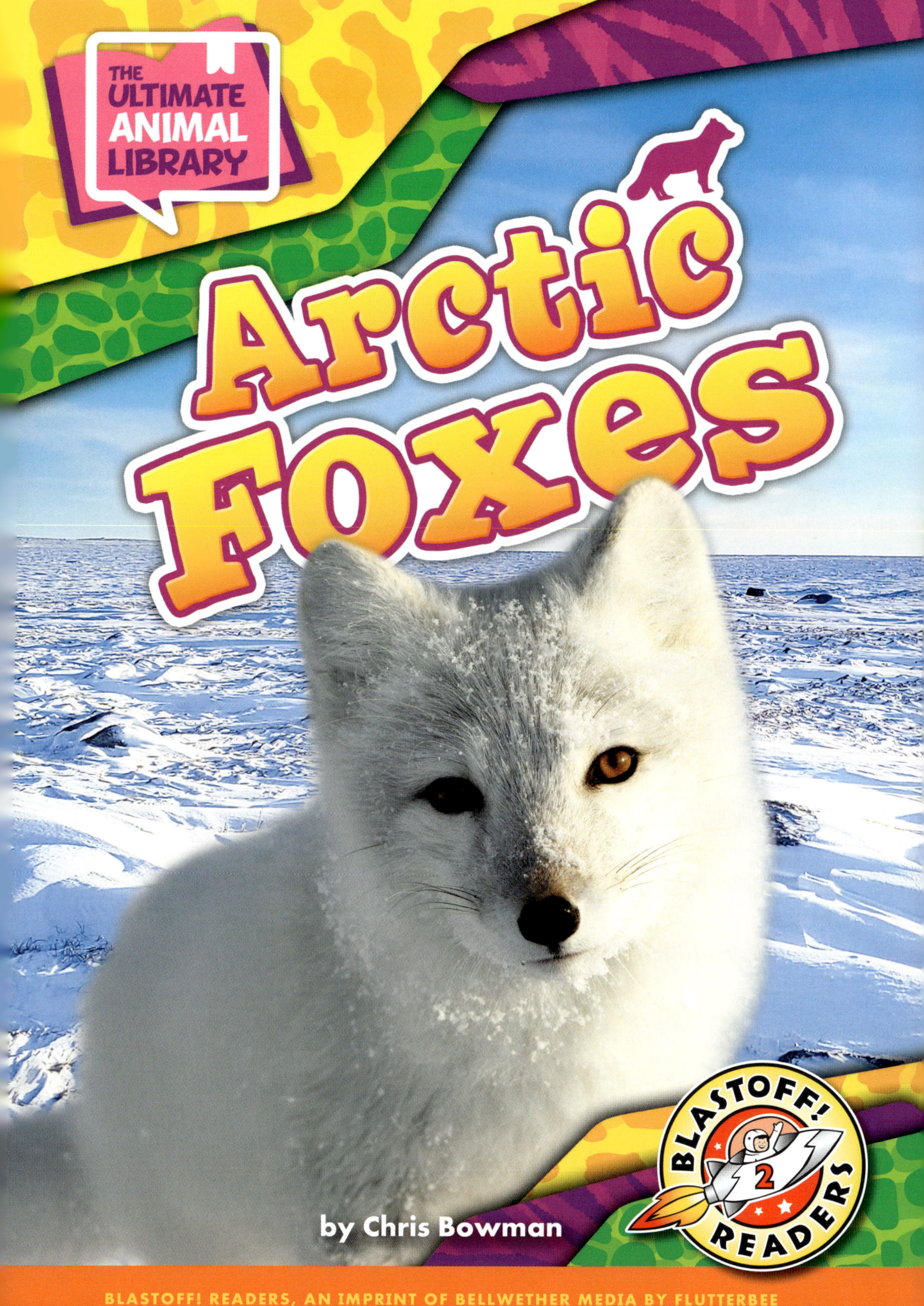

BLASTOFF! READERS, AN IMPRINT OF BELLWETHER MEDIA BY FLUTTERBEE

**Blastoff! Readers** are carefully developed by literacy experts to build reading stamina and move students toward fluency by combining standards-based content with developmentally appropriate text.

**Level 1** provides the most support through repetition of high-frequency words, light text, predictable sentence patterns, and strong visual support.

**Level 2** offers early readers a bit more challenge through varied sentences, increased text load, and text-supportive special features.

**Level 3** advances early-fluent readers toward fluency through increased text load, less reliance on photos, advancing concepts, longer sentences, and more complex special features.

**★ Blastoff! Universe**

This edition first published in 2026 by Bellwether Media, Inc.



For information regarding permission, write to Bellwether Media, Inc., Attention: Permissions Department, 3500 American Blvd W, Suite 150, Bloomington, MN 55431.

Library of Congress Cataloging-in-Publication Data is available at www.loc.gov or upon request from the publisher.

ISBN: 9798893047882 (hardcover)
ISBN: 9798893048889 (ebook)

Editor: Kieran Downs Designer: Brittany McIntosh

Printed in the United States of America, North Mankato, MN.

# Table of Contents

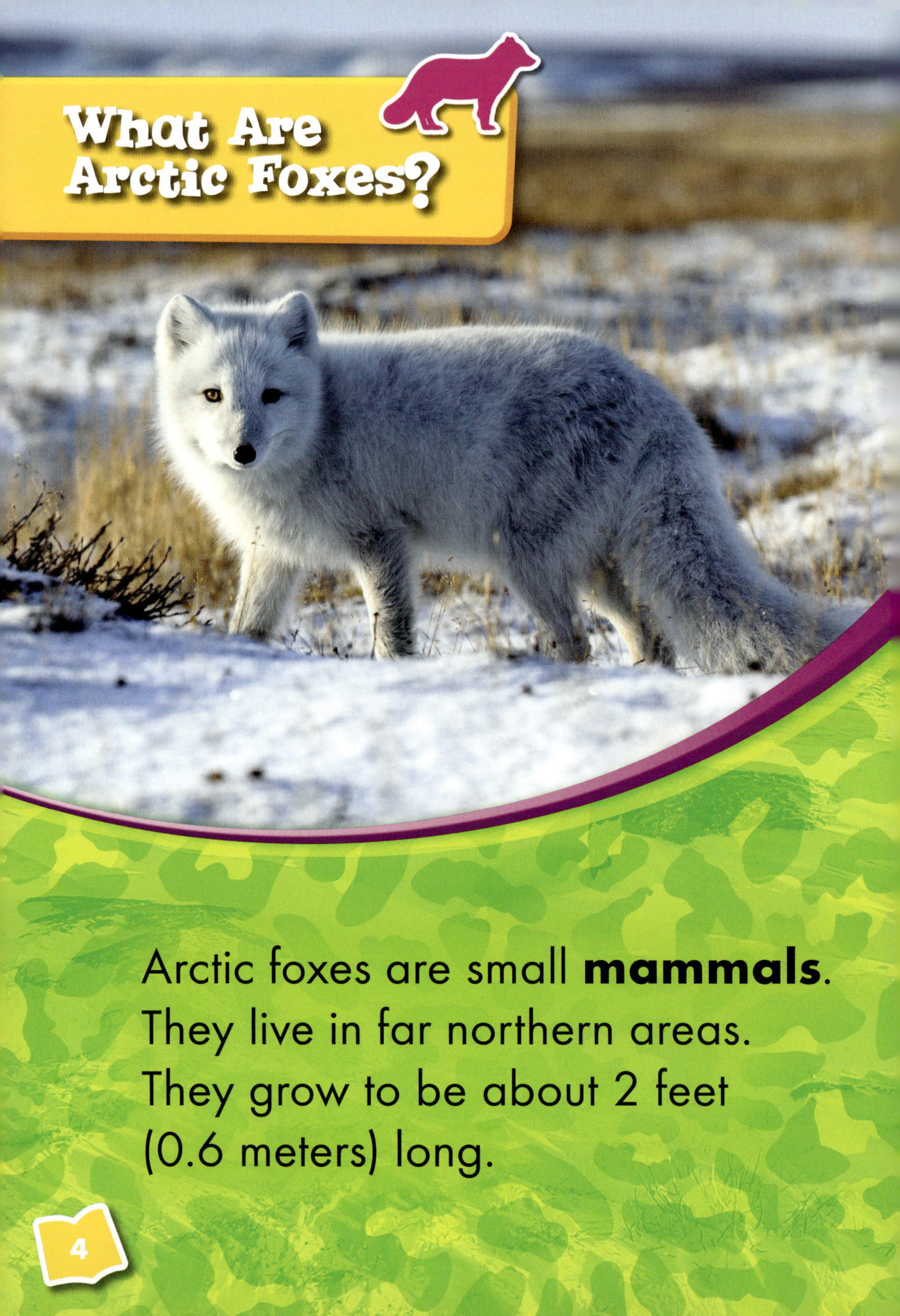

# What Are Arctic Foxes?

Arctic foxes are small **mammals**. They live in far northern areas. They grow to be about 2 feet (0.6 meters) long.

# Arctic Fox Report

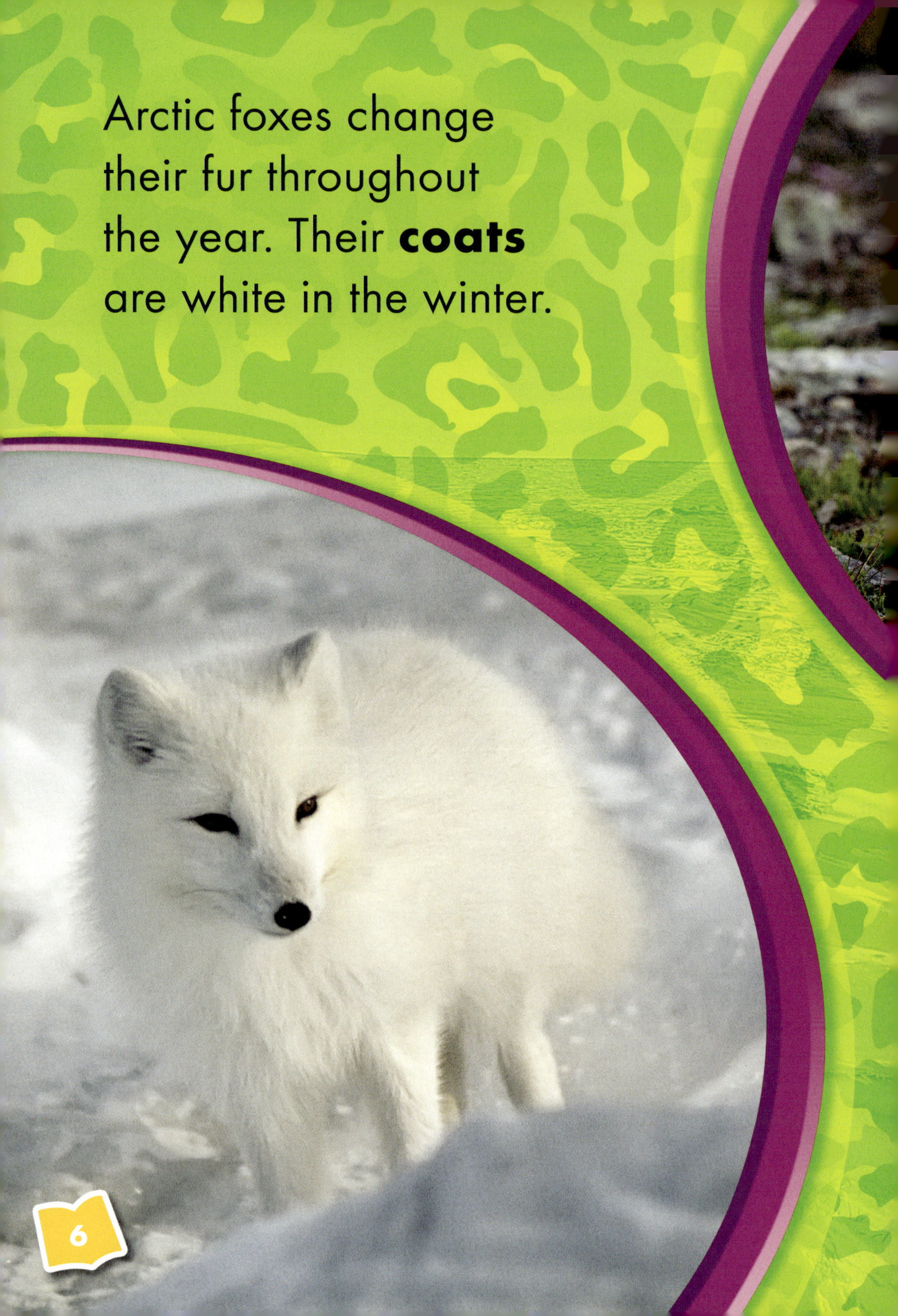

Arctic foxes change their fur throughout the year. Their **coats** are white in the winter.

Their fur is brown or gray
in warmer months.

Arctic foxes have short legs.

Their paws grow thick fur in the winter. This keeps their toes warm and helps them **grip** ice.

Arctic foxes have short **snouts** and small ears.

They have fluffy tails. Their tails can be over 1 foot (0.3 meters) long.

# Spot an Arctic Fox

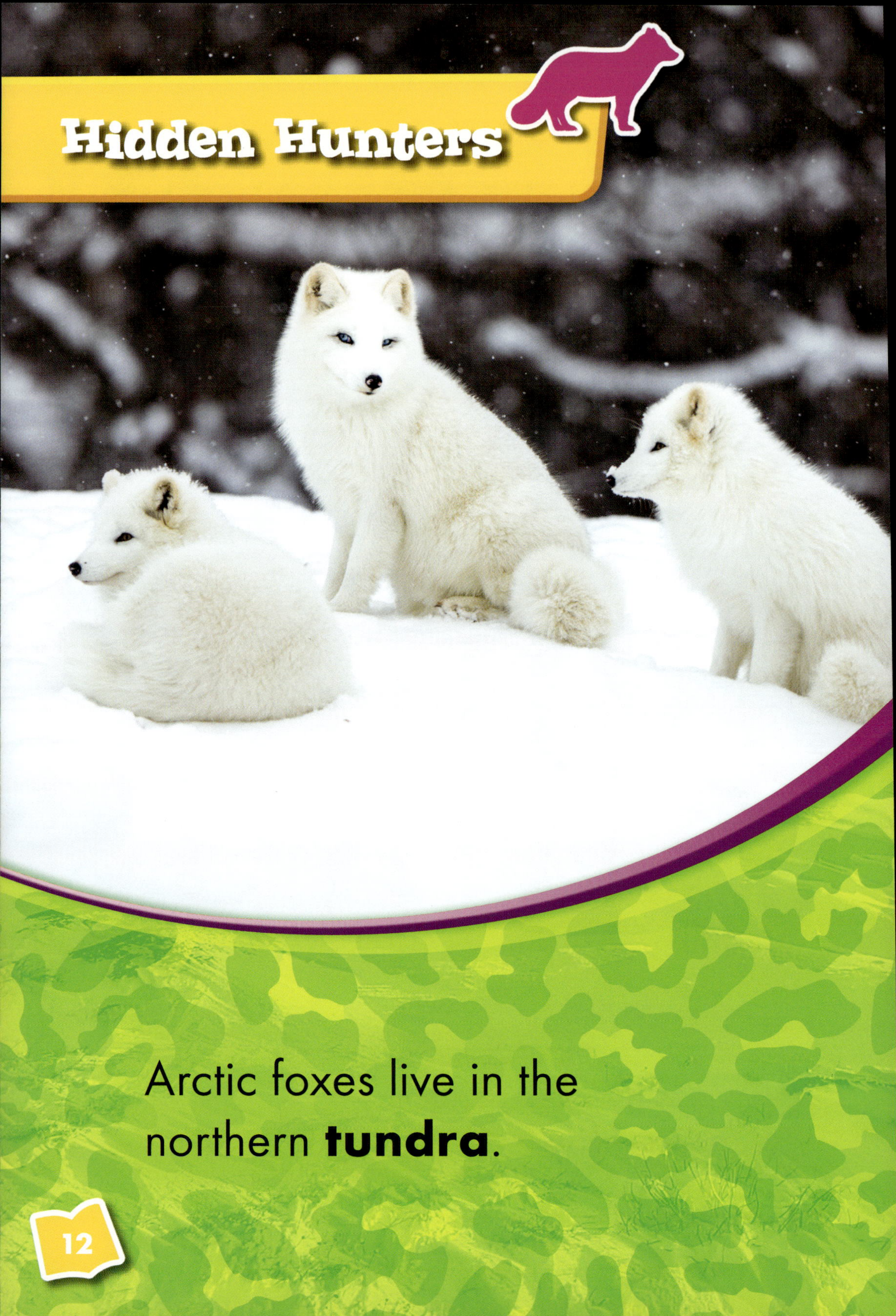

## Hidden Hunters

Arctic foxes live in the northern **tundra**.

They live with a family group during the **breeding** season. Some **dens** have been used for many years!

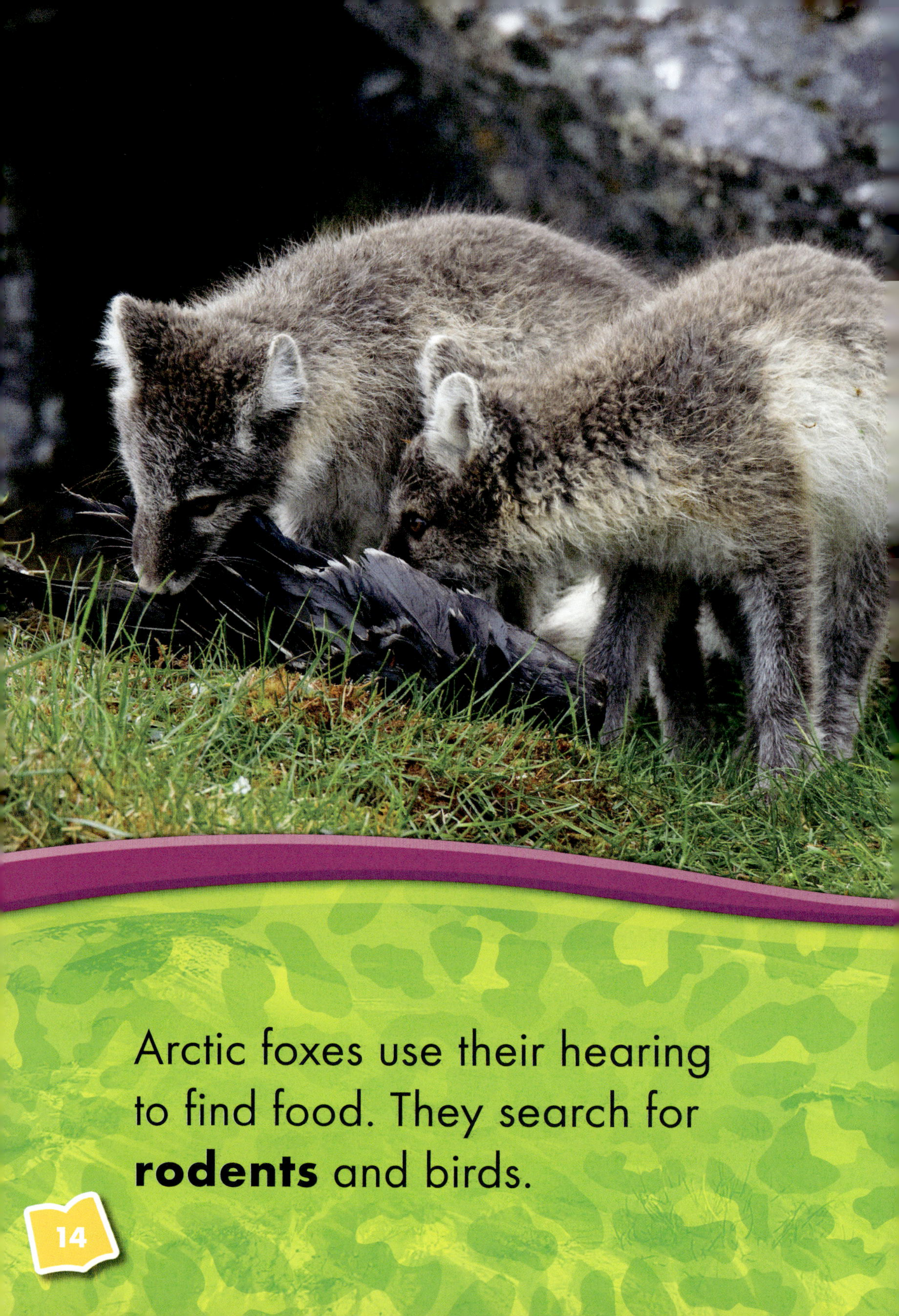

Arctic foxes use their hearing to find food. They search for **rodents** and birds.

They also eat berries and **insects**.

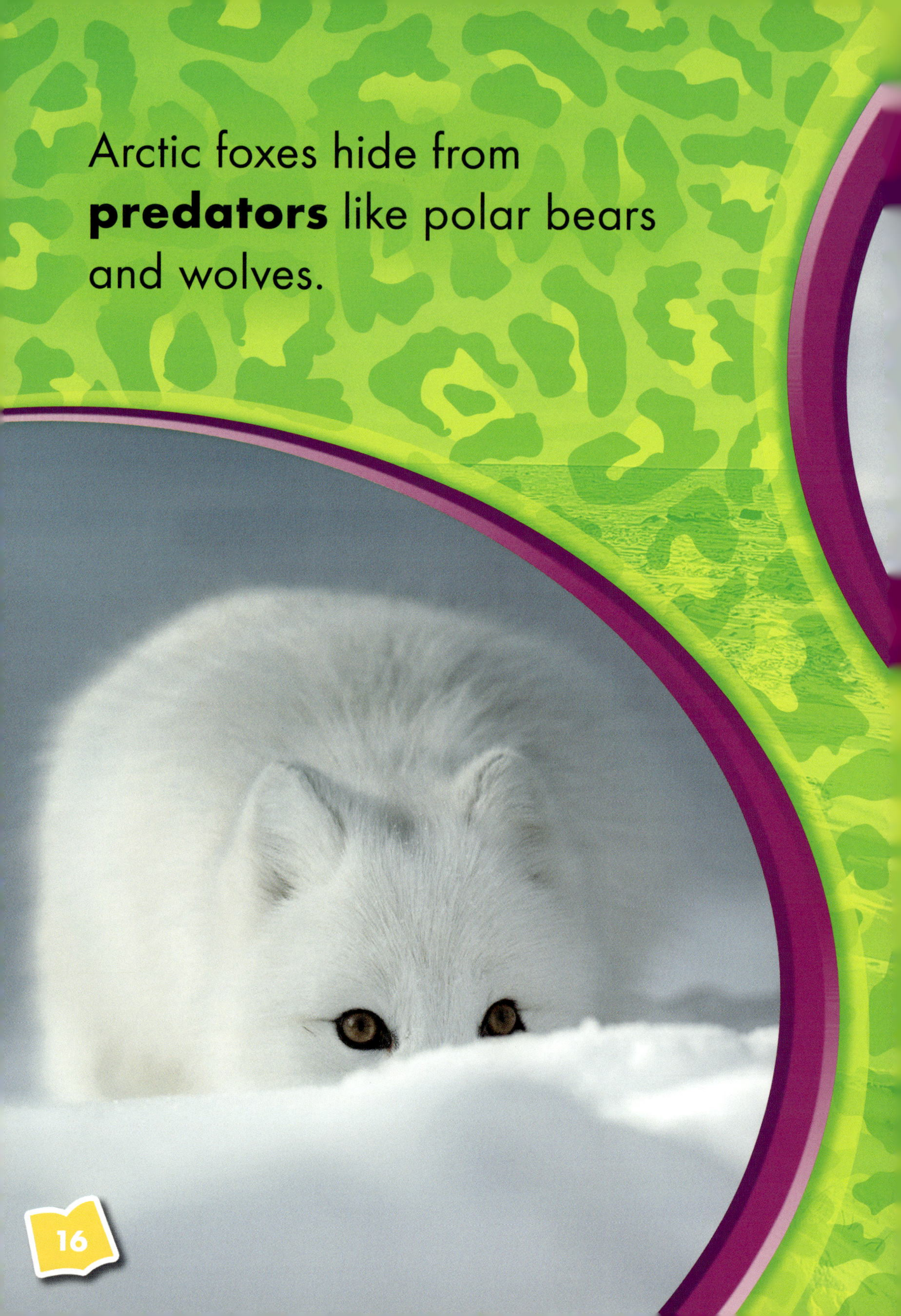

Arctic foxes hide from **predators** like polar bears and wolves.

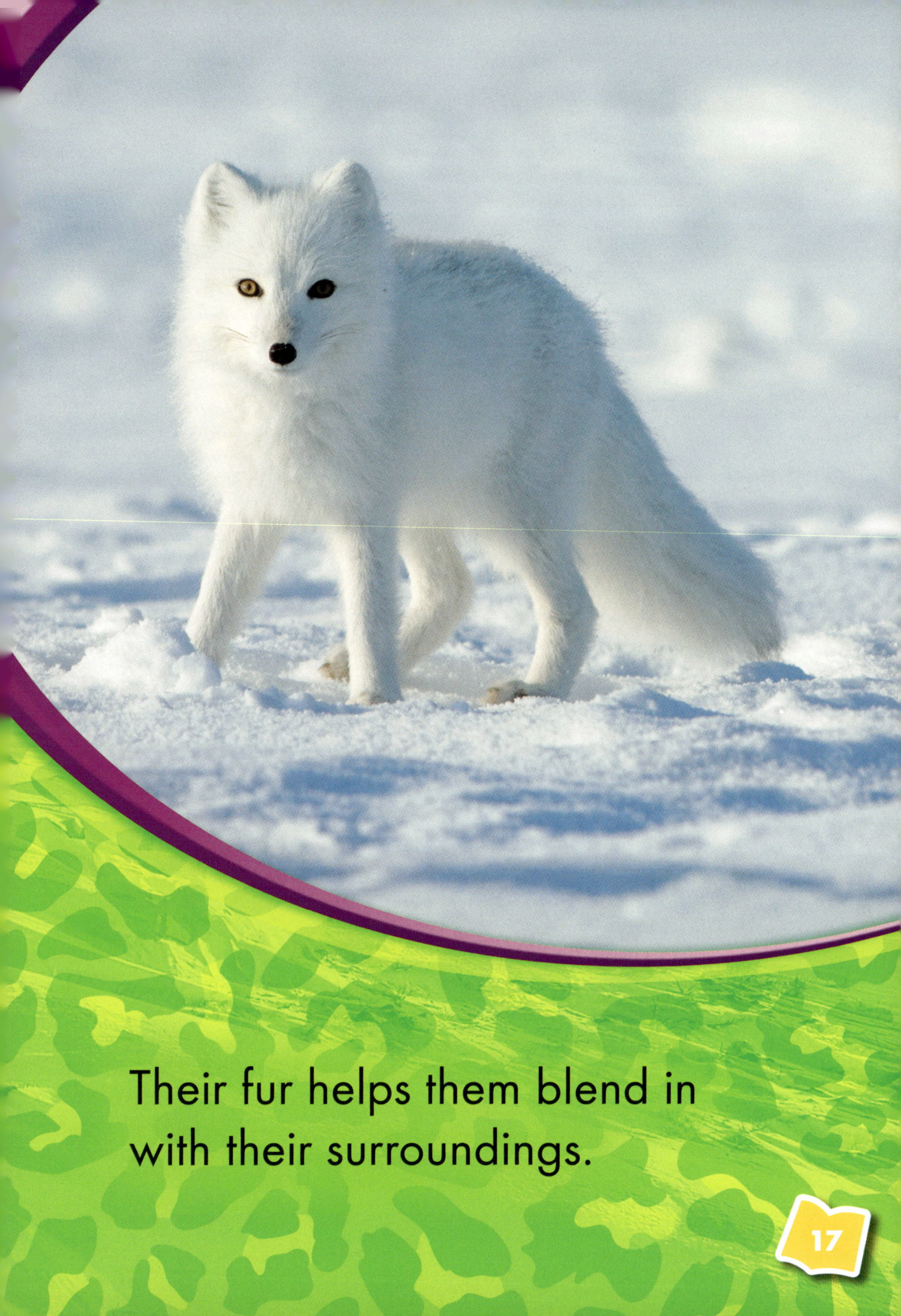

Their fur helps them blend in with their surroundings.

## Growing Up

Female arctic foxes have up to 25 **pups** at once. Most **litters** have between 5 and 11 pups.

Both parents help care for the pups.

pup

Arctic fox pups **nurse** for about one month. Then they learn to hunt.

Pups go off on their own after about five months. Time to find a new den!

## Life of an Arctic Fox

**Name of Babies**

pups

**Number of Babies**

up to 25

**Time Spent with Parents**

about 5 months

**Life Span**

# Glossary

**breeding**—related to producing offspring

**coats**—the hair or fur covering an animal

**dens**—sheltered places

**grip**—to hold tightly

**insects**—small animals with six legs and bodies divided into three parts

**litters**—groups of babies born at the same time

**mammals**—warm-blooded animals that have backbones and feed their young milk

**nurse**—to drink mom's milk

**predators**—animals that hunt other animals for food

**pups**—baby arctic foxes

**rodents**—small animals that gnaw on their food

**snouts**—the noses and mouths of some animals

**tundra**—flat, treeless, frozen land found in far northern regions

# To Learn More

## AT THE LIBRARY

Bowman, Chris. *Red Foxes*. Minneapolis, Minn.: Bellwether Media, 2025.

Neuenfeldt, Elizabeth. *Arctic Animals*. Minneapolis, Minn.: Bellwether Media, 2023.

Perish, Patrick. *Red Foxes*. Minneapolis, Minn.: Bellwether Media, 2022.

## ON THE WEB

**FACTSURFER**

Factsurfer.com gives you a safe, fun way to find more information.

1. Go to www.factsurfer.com.
2. Enter "arctic foxes" into the search box and click 🔍.
3. Select your book cover to see a list of related content.

# Index

The images in this book are reproduced through the courtesy of: DmitryND, front cover (fox), p. 10; Derek Robbins, front cover (background), pp. 2-3; Roi Shomer, p. 3; Alexey Seafarer, p. 4; outdoorsman, p. 6; Charles Bergman, p. 7; Josef Pittner, p. 8; NaturesMomentsuk, p. 9; JoannaPerchaluk, pp. 10-11; Eric Isselee, p. 11; Glass and Nature, p. 12; imageBROKER.com/ Alamy Stock Photo, p. 13; Arterra Picture Library/ Alamy Stock Photo, pp. 14-15, 18-19; Lumin Heart Studio, p. 15 (polar bears); photomaster, p. 15 (wolves); Holly S Cannon, p. 15 (foxes); Nick Pecker, p. 15 (rodents); AndreAnita, p. 15 (birds); Andrew Astbury, p. 16; Steven J. Kazlowski/ Alamy Stock Photo, p. 17; Menno Schaefer, p. 18; Dgwildlife, pp. 20, 21; David Boutin, p. 23.